LETTER

FROM A

BLACKSMITH,

TO THE

MINISTERS and ELDERS

OF THE

CHURCH of SCOTLAND.

In which the Manner of PUBLIC WORSHIP in that CHURCH is confidered ; its Inconveniencies and Defects pointed out ; and Methods for removing them humbly propofed.

Be not rafh with thy mouth, and let not thine heart be hafty to utter any thing before God: for God is in Heaven, and thou upon Earth : therefore let thy words be few.

Eccl. v. 2.

I will pray with the Spirit, and I will pray with the underftanding alfo.

1 Cor. xiv. 15.

THE FOURTH EDITION.

DUBLIN:

Printed by GEORGE FAULKNER in *Effex-Street,*

M. DCC. LIX.

ADVERTISEMENT

FROM THE

LONDON EDITOR.

IF, in the following sheets, the reader finds the Blacksmith now and then introducing scraps of Latin, he will be the less surprized if he reflects, that in Scotland most of the mechanics have a smattering of that language, which is taught even in the country parish schools. It seems the author thought it incumbent upon him, when he had to do with the clergy, to muster up all the little learning he was master of. With what propriety and judgment his quotations are introduced, is submitted to the reader, by his most obedient servant,

The PUBLISHER.

A LETTER

TO THE

MINISTERS and ELDERS

OF THE

CHURCH of SCOTLAND.

Right Reverend and Right Honourable,

I Have prefumed to addrefs you upon a fubject, which appears to me of the greateft importance, and worthy of the confideration of the minifters and elders of the church of Scotland; thank God, I have reafon to hope, from your wifdom, learning, and piety, that I fhall be favoured with a fair and patient hearing, tho' my fphere in life be low, and my fentiments fet off with no other advantages than fincerity and truth, as far as I can diftinguifh it; for God, and my own heart, bear witnefs, that I prefent this addrefs with no other view than to pro-mote (as much as I can) the glory of God, the in-terefts of true religion, and the honour, purity, and peace of the church of Scotland. Could I have found any better method of communicating my

thoughts

thoughts than by a letter, I would willingly have chofen it ; or had I hoped ever to have feen a more favourable feafon than the prefent, I would patiently have waited for it. But now we are bleffed with a learned body of clergy, with a prince well difpofed to promote true piety among his people, and we have the happinefs to live in an age, in which the prejudices of parties are moftly worn off, the rage of difpute abated, and men difpofed to hear truth, and obey reafon ; fuch peaceful happy days are defigned by heaven, and ought to be employed by men, to repair in religion, what has been pulled down by mad paffions, in turbulent times ; to reftore to its firft beauty, whatever has been defaced by party prejudices in the days of contention, and to recover the purity of our faith, and decency of our worfhip, from the ruft and low fuperftition which they have contracted in the ignorant ages ; and tinctures of enthufiafm they imbibed in the fhock and tumult of the reformation. There was no church that met with greater oppofition, or was more violently agitated than ours ; and tho' (thank God) it ftood out the ftorm, yet it fuffered very feverely ; and when the fury was in fome degree abated, and men had time to look about them, our church appeared little better than a ruin ; her facred buildings levelled with the ground, or bare fhattered walls, the ftanding monuments of religious madnefs ; her treafures robbed by facrilegious hands ; her regifters deftroyed, or carried off ; her funds applied to profane ufes ; and her clergy left to ftarve : would to God fhe had fuffered only in thefe lefs effential things.

But along with thefe fhe contracted a fingular and whimfical tafte, her principles of faith grew dark and myfterious, and her method of worfhip defective and unreafonable ; fome of thefe ruins fhe never can repair; fome of them indeed time has in a great meafure patched up ; and fome of them remain to be repaired by the prefent rulers of our church, or by fucceeding generations : of this kind is our publick worfhip ; in which there are feveral things that demand your ferious attention, and call loudly for the diligence and learning of the prefent age. I will prefume, with due deference, to point out a few of them ; hoping that my poor endeavours may at leaft obtain pardon, out of refpect to the importance of the fubject, and the fincerity of my intention ; and that fome able head and good heart, will take the hint, and fully point out the flaws, in our prefent way of worfhip, and direct us how to amend them. Some unprejudiced, and happy genius may perhaps appear, whofe perfuafive eloquence, refined expreffion, and conclufive arguments may command attention, and gain affent; in fpite of the bigotry of the ignorant, the vain ambition of thofe, that are fond of popularity, and the whimfical opinions of enthufiafts. 'Till fuch an one fhall appear, I hope you will not take it amifs, that I offer my remarks, efpecially as I beg leave to affure you, that this my addrefs does not proceed from a fondnefs of novelty, much lefs any intention to difturb the peace of the church eftablifhed by law, or indeed from any other or any worfe motive, than that her publick fervice may be fuch as feems beft calculated for promoting the interefts of religion and virtue ; and moft fuitable for reafonable creatures to offer, and an infinitely wife God to accept.

FIRST, I fubmit to your ferious confideration, whether a larger portion of the fcriptures fhould not be read every Lord's day in our publick affemblies ; the reading of the fcriptures always made a part of the publick fervice in all the

churches

churches of God ; the law and the prophets, were
folemnly read * in the fynagogues every fabbath
day ; our Saviour countenanced and fanctified this
practice † with his prefence and example; the
apoftle Paul peremptorily commands Timothy to
give attendance to reading, as well as to exhortation and doctrine ; and the primitive church re-
ligioufly obferved this command, as Juftin Mar-
tyr ‖ bears witnefs. "Upon the day that is called
Sunday (fays he) all that live in the country, or
in the towns, affemble in one place, and the
commentaries of the apoftles, or the writings of the
prophets are read, 'till the time allotted for them be
expired." Nay more, our own directory for
Public worfhip, (which perhaps may have more
weight with fome, than the example of our Saviour,
the command of his apoftles, or the practice of
the pureft antiquity, recommends that ordinarily
one chapter out of each Teftament fhould be read
at every meeting. I am at a lofs whether to
afcribe the negligence of this effential part of our
fervice to the pride of the clergy, or the perverfe-
nefs of the people, perhaps it may be in fome
degree owing to both ; the clergy, probably, think
that it would not give them a fufficient opportunity
to difplay their own talents ; and the people, that
it does not fo fully pleafe their ears, always itching
with the defire of fomething new: to the firft I
fhall only obferve, that tho' we have, as we always
ought to have, a very great refpect for the ob-
fervations and difcourfes of our fpiritual guides,
yet at the fame time we cannot but wifh to hear
what the *Spirit faith unto the churches*, in his own
words; we have room to wifh for this, as we are
told

---

* Acts xv. 28. † Luke iv. 17. ‖ Apol. ii. p. 28. Tertul.
ad gent. pag. 47. § 498.

told by the apoftle, that the fcriptures *are profitable for doctrine, for reproof, for correction, for inftruction in righteoufnefs*; and that by them *the man of God may be perfect, thoroughly furnifhed unto all good works.* It is true you indulge us now and then with ten or a dozen of verfes of pure fcripture in our publick affemblies, but as we * have no regular plan of reading the fcriptures, of confequence we only hear detached places, chofen at the pleafure of the preacher, and applied to what purpofes he thinks fit; this leaves our underftandings too much in the power of the clergy, and expofes the fimple and ignorant (who make the greateft part of our congregations) to be feduced by the party principles and whimfical opinions of the preacher. It may at firft fight appear, that the whole plan of our worfhip is as happily calculated for making a property of the laity, and keeping their judgements and confciences in the power of the parfon, as any part of the popifh fyftem; for the minifter needs not read any part of the fcriptures unlefs he pleafes; he may chufe what place he thinks proper, may begin where he inclines, and break off when he has a mind; he may mangle them in any manner he thinks fit, and make them fay whatever he would have them to fay.

But allow me to tell you, that as the reading of the fcriptures in public affemblies is of divine appointment, no power upon earth can difpenfe with the obligation; as they contain the articles of our faith, and the rules by which we are to regulate our lives, nothing can fupply, and therefore nothing ought to ufurp their place; and as all
the

---

* Our directory declares that it is requifite that all the cannonical books be read over in order; but our parfons proceed in a different method.

the reformed churches are agreed, that the fcriptures are plain in things neceffary to falvation, we ought to hear them as they are, without your gloffes and comments ; nay, what can be more effectual for our falvation, or fo proper for Inftruction, feeing they bear witnefs for themfelves, that the *word of God is fharper than a two-edged fword, piercing even to the dividing afunder of the foul and fpirit, and is a difcerner of the thoughts and intents of the heart* *. *That it converts the foul, and makes the fimple wife* †. Is there any thing that can be fubftituted in the place of the fcriptures, from which, fuch great and happy effects may be expected ? But if this fhameful negligence be owing to the perverfe humour of the people, who perhaps may think that the reading of the fcriptures is a dry infipid part of the fervice, you will not, I hope, take it ill if I fay, that amufements are more their errand to church than inftruction, that they are more defirous of new words than found doctrine, and that in fact their hearts are carnal, and eftranged from the things of the Spirit ; for the apoftle informs us, that the natural man receiveth not the things of the Spirit, for they are foolifhnefs to him. Pardon me if I think that your compliance with this humour is like Aaron's to the folly of the Ifraelites ; as he fet up a calf made with his own hands, to be the object of the people's worfhip, inftead of the living God ; fo you fet up your own compofitions, to direct the faith and regulate the manners of the people, in the place of the fcriptures of truth, dictated by the Holy Spirit. The fervice of God in the way of his own appointment ever was, and ever will be difliked by the bulk of the people ; the Jews would willingly have embraced any religion, but that

which

---

* Heb. iv 12.   † Pfal. xix. 7.

which was given them from heaven; they would have facrificed in any place but in that pointed out by their Maker; and thought no rites burdenfome but thofe that God was pleafed to appoint; but with refpect to thofe the prophet upbraids them with faying, as our people fay, *Behold, what a wearinefs is it* *. It is the bufinefs and duty of minifters to check and refift this humour of the people, and not encourage it by a mean compliance with a vitiated tafte, and a bafe betraying of the truft repofed in them; but, alas! the tafte of the people in this coincides with the inclinations of the paftor, and flatters his pride and vanity too much to be reftrained; however, with all humility I prefume to beg, that you would be pleafed to confider, how you can anfwer to God, to your own confciences, and to us your hearers, for fuch a dangerous and wilful neglect.

As to praife, we feem to ftudy to give this part of our worfhip as much the air of rufticity, and contempt of God as poffible; becaufe we thought that the engagement of the heart was (as indeed it is) the effence of this part of worfhip, we have whimfically thrown out every thing that helped to engage and elevate the heart; many of the words we ufe are obfolete and low, the verfification is mean and barbarous, and the mufick harfh and ill performed; our harmony, otherways not very fweet, is entirely loft, and the fenfe broke off at every line; our pofture too is the moft indecent, negligent, and improper for finging well, that we could have contrived; it is true the pofture is of no importance, farther than as it expreffeth our reverence to the God whom we worfhip: yet it is as neceffary that it fhould be decent, as that our words fhould be proper, for both are only figns
of

* Malachi i. 13

of inward fenfations; fhould we find a fellow crying very bitterly, and dancing very brifkly, thefe are figns of fo oppofite fenfations, that we would be apt to imagine that he was diftracted; and what fhall we conclude, when we hear a congregation addreffing God in fome ardent hymn, or earneft petition, and fee them fitting upon their breech, or lolling with the moft negligent air and pofture upon their feats? the figns here point to very different fenfations! Quintillian feems to think that there may be a folecifm in gefture as well as in the expreffion; and if fuch a thing can be, we feem guilty of a very great one, in ufing the moft indifferent, negligent pofture, when we are employed in the moft interefting and ferious affair, I mean offering praife to the living God.

I cannot help thinking, that all the rational people of our communion muft be fhocked with the indecencies, and follies, that attend the adminiftration of our Lord's fupper, known among the common people by the name of an *occafion*. We accufe the Roman church of fuperftition, and that very juftly; but in this inftance fhe may fairly retort and tell us, that we blame in others, what we approve of, or at leaft allow in ourfelves; for if our people did not imagine that there was fome fuperior virtue, in fermons preached upon thefe *occafions*, fome fanctity in the place, or fome merit in their attendance, it is unlikely that fuch Numbers, who have no intention to communicate, fhould crowd from all quarters, leave their parifh churches almoft empty, and flight as good fermons, which they might hear without the fatigue of travelling, or the inconveniencies that attend a crowd. Superftition in all countries has the fame effect, tho' it may be directed to different objects: in popifh countries, people crowd from place to place to vifit the

fhrines

shrines of the faints, and pray before the moft famous images; in Scotland, they run from kirk to kirk as it were after the hoft, and fiock to fee a facrament, as thofe to fhare in a proceffion; and too many of our people (with fhame we muft confefs) make the fame ufe of our *occafions*, that the papifts do of their pilgrimages and proceffions; that is, to indulge themfelves in drunkennefs, luft, and idlenefs; moft of the fervants when they agree to ferve their mafters in the weftern parts of the kingdom, make a fpecial provifion, that they fhall have liberty to go to a certain number of fairs, or to an equal number of *facraments*; and as they confider a *facrament* or an *occafion* (as they call the adminiftration of the Lord's fupper in a neighbouring parifh) in the fame light in which they do a fair, fo they behave at it much in the fame manner. I defy Italy, in fpite of all its fuperftition, to produce a fcene better fitted to raife pity and regret in a religious, humane, and underftanding heart, or to afford an ampler field for ridicule, to the carelefs and profane, than what they call a field preaching upon one of thofe *occafions*: at the time of the adminiftration of our Lord's fupper (ye know) that upon the Thurfday, Saturday, and Monday, we have preaching in the fields near the church, which it feems we muft not ufe upon that *occafion*; I have often thought that the frequency of the fight makes it familiar, and confequently lefs fhocking to you, or that being in the inner circle, you feldom have accefs to fee the indecency and abfurdity of the whole fcene, otherways you would not encourage it. Allow me then to defcribe it, as it really is: at firft you find a great number of men and women lying together upon the grafs; here they are fleeping and fnoring, fome with their faces towards heaven, others with their faces turned
down-

downwards, or covered with their bonnets; there you find a knot of young fellows and girls making affignations to go home together in the evening, or to meet in fome ale-houfe; in another place you fee a pious circle fitting round an ale barrel, many of which ftand ready upon carts, for the refrefhment of the faints. The heat of the fummer feafon, the fatigue of travelling, and the greatnefs of the crowd naturally difpofe them to drink; which inclines fome of them to fleep, works up the enthufiafm of others, and contributes not a little to produce thofe miraculous converfions that fometimes happen at thefe *occafions*; in a word, in this *facred* affembly there is an odd mixture of religion, fleep, drinking, courtfhip, and a confufion of fexes, ages, and characters. When you get a litttle nearer the fpeaker, fo as to be within the reach of the found, tho' not of the fenfe of the words, for that can only reach a fmall circle, even when the preacher is favoured with a calm; and when there happens to be any wind ftirring, hardly can one fentence be heard diftinctly at any confiderable diftance; in this fecond circle you will find fome weeping, and others laughing, fome preffing to get nearer the tent or tub in which the parfon is fweating, bawling, jumping, and beating the defk; others fainting with the ftifling heat, or wreftling to extricate themfelves from the crowd; one feems very devout and ferious, and the next moment is fcolding and curfing his neighbour, for fqueezing or treading on him; in an inftant after, his countenance is compofed to the religious gloom, and he is groaning, fighing, and weeping for his fins; in a word, there is fuch an abfurd mixture of the ferious and comick, that were we conveened for any other purpofe, than that of worfhipping the God and

govern-

governor of nature, the scene would exceed *all power of face*.

BUT when one considers, what solemn awe should accompany the pronounciation of his name, and what decent gravity attend his worship, and sees such an unhappy contrast, if his heart be not entirely unacquainted with the feelings of humanity, the sigh will force its way, and the pitying tear start into his eye ; especially if he knows, that many of the clergy encourage this absurdity ; that this is the time, when they vie with one another for popularity, and try who can conveen the greatest mob ; that some of the elders are so fond of these religious farces, that they have threatened to abandon their churches, if the absurd practice of preaching without doors should be discontinued ; and that even those of the clergy, who have sense to perceive its inconveniencies, and ingenuity to own that it is wrong, yet want courage to oppose the popular phrensy, and resolution to reform what in their own hearts they cannot but condemn. Whether we consider this practice in a moral, political, or religious light, we shall find it attended with very bad consequences ; how much must it encourage drunkenness when such crowds are conveened, from all quarters ; what must the consequence be, when a whole country side is thrown loose, and young fellows and girls are going home together by night, in the gayest season of the year ; when every thing naturally inspires warm desires, and silence, secresy, and darkness encourage them ? When I was a young fellow at my apprenticeship, I was a great frequenter of these *occasions*, and know them so well, that whatever others may think, I would not chuse a wife that had often frequented them, nor trust a daughter too much among those rambling saints ; old maids

may

may perhaps be allowed to revenge themselves of the world, by growing religious at the easy rate of running from sacrament to sacrament; and they who are in pain to be provided with husbands, may possibly find their account in frequenting those *sacred* assemblies; but I would advise others to go but seldom, and never to a greater distance than that they can return before sun-set; lest by frequenting them too much, they contract an idle disposition of mind, and by staying too late, they get into a *bad habit of body*. Nor are the consequences of this practice considered in a political light, more favourable than in a moral; our church disclaims all holy days, and I should offend at once against truth and the rules of our church, if I said that we observe any such; but I presume that the number of our idle days will fall very little short of that number in the popish kalendar, and all the difference is, that their holy days are fixt, and, our idle days moveable; theirs are dedicated to some saint, and ours are devoted to some *occasion*; theirs foster superstition and idleness, and so do ours; theirs are signalized now and then by miraculous cures, by which the patient's health is seldom bettered; and ours by miraculous conversions *, by which the convert's morals are rarely mended; and to do the papists justice they deal more fairly in their miracles than we, for a man can see if a crooked limb be made straight, because it is the object of the sense, but a miracle wrought instantaneously in the mind, must be taken upon the word of the patient or the parson; but the truth is, their holy days, and our idle days, whatever miracles they may produce, do hurt to true religion: the people lose many labouring days by them, and the country

—————————————

* See two volumes published at Glasgow by M. Gillies.

country is deprived of the fruit of their industry. I have seen above three thousand people at one of these *occasions*; but supposing that one with another there are only fifteen hundred, and that each of them one with another might earn sixpence a day, every sacrament, by its three idle days, will cost the country much about 112*l.* 10*s. Sterling*, not including the days that they who live at a great distance must lose in coming and going, nor the losses the farmer must sustain, when *occasions* happen in the hay, harvest or seed-times; the man of business, when they chance to fall upon the market days; or the tradesman when any particular piece of work is in hand that requires dispatch: now supposing the sacrament should be administred only twice a year, in all our churches, which if it be not, it ought to be, these *occasions*, as they are managed at present, will cost Scotland at least 235,000*l. Sterling*, an immense sum for sermons! the greatest part of which might be saved, much disorder and irregularity prevented, would the assembly be graciously pleased to appoint some particular Sundays in the four seasons *, for the administration of this sacrament, over all the kingdom. We were too fond of novelties, and perhaps established practices founded on reason, and approved by long experience; and we could hardly have pitched upon a more unnatural method than the present, consider it in what light you will; for if the design of this sacrament, next to setting forth the death of our Lord, be to remain as a pledge of love and charity among christians, it does not with us seem at all to answer the design;

as

* This was the method for several years about the time of the reformation.

as our congregations like difcontented children, take
a private hour as it were, and eat their bread by
themfelves in a corner; whereas all the reft of
the chriftian world, do chriftian like communicate
together three times in the year; and as they fhew
forth the fame meritorious death, they fhew it
forth at the fame feafon, and like brethren fit down
at once to the fame love feaft.

But befides this, the great noife that we make
about thefe *occafions*, leads our people to lay too
great a ftrefs upon them, and to imagine that there
is fomething meritorious, nay, that the life of religion lies in hearing a great number of facramental
fermons, they ferve nearly the fame ends in our
church, that confeflion, and abfolution, do among
the papifts; our people put on a very demure look
fome days before the facrament; the gloom gra-
dually gathers upon their faces as it approaches;
and they look like criminals going to execution
when the day is come; juft fo may it be feen in
popifh countries, in the feafons fet apart for confeflion and penance; but in both countries the
profeffed repentance proves only a flafh of devotion,
and as matters were made up with the Deity, and
all former accounts cleared, the papift foon puts
off his penitential countenance, and the Prefbyterian
lays by his facramental face, and they and we in
a little time are the fame men that we were before.

And as thefe *occafions* make our people lay too
great a ftrefs upon the outward means, while they
neglect the great end of all religion, I mean to better
the heart, and reform the conduct; fo they raife
contention, heart burnings, envy, and factions
among our clergy, while they contend for popularity, vie with one another who fhall conveen the
greateft crowd, and work up the mob to the
higheft pitch of enthufiafm; and they often fucceed

fo well, that they bring the weak and ignorant, to the very brink of downright madnefs. I have feen fcenes of this nature, that had much more of the fury of the bacchanalia, than the calm, ferious, fincere devotion of a chriftian facrament. It is here that the minifters difplay the falfe eloquence which catches the crowd, and confifts in a ftrong voice, a melancholy tone, and thundering out at random damnation, death, and hell-fire, and flames, devils, darknefs and gnafhing of teeth; any one who has good lungs, and can borrow the beggar's cant, and the merry Andrew's action, may become very popular, and make a great figure at an *occafion* : for the contention there is not, who fhall reafon moft juftly, deliver moft gracefully, or direct their difcourfe in the beft manner for bettering the heart, and reforming the manners of the audience; but who fhall appear more frantick, cry loudeft, fpeak with the deepeft, ftrangeft and moft hollow tone; and be moft wrapt up in myftery, and fcholaftick terms. I have known thefe qualifications make nonfenfe triumph over fenfe, ignorance be preferred to learning; and incoherent, unintelligible, and contradictory rhapfodies, be received with admiration by the gazing crowd; while plain, learned, and pious fermons, delivered with a becoming modefty and gravity, have been preached almoft to the empty pews. Quintilian, affigning the reafons why the ignorant orators were heard with more applaufe by the mob, than the ingenious and learned, paints fo juftly the methods by which our minifters contend for popularity at the *occafions,* that the paffage is worth tranfcribing, *Clamant ubique, et omnia levata (ut ipfi dicunt) manu emugiunt, multo difcurfu, anhelitu, jactatione, gefta, motuque capitis furentes—mire ad pullatum circulum facit—cum ille eruditus modeftus et effe, et videri malit—at illi hanc*

B   *vim-*

vim appellant, que eſt potius violentia *. The art of managing mankind (ſays Mr. Addiſon, ſpeaking of quacks in phyſick) is only to make them ſtare a little, to keep up their aſtoniſhment and to let nothing be familiar to them; this art is perfectly well underſtood by our parſons, for at theſe *occa-ſions*, they try who ſhall make the people ſtare moſt; and ſometimes they make them ſtare ſo long and ſo eagerly, that the poor people turn almoſt ſtark ſtaring mad : we are damned an hundred times over in one day; and damned too, without any ſort of diſcretion; for moſt of our miniſters that I have had occaſion to hear, ſeem to have embraced, and to certainly propagate, Hoadly's notions of the ſacrament of the ſupper; and yet they go on damning us ſtill, when their maſter ſays, and they ſometimes ſay, that the communion is little more than a mere ceremony. Poor lay men I own ought not to preſume to dictate to the parſon, what notions he is to embrace, and teach; but I humbly hope that we have a right to expect that the parſon be conſiſtent with himſelf, ſo far at leaſt as not to damn us, where at other times he teaches us that there is no danger.

But as it is not likely that theſe opportunities of ſpeaking *great and ſwelling words* † will be given up, while men are ſo *preſumptious and ſelf-willed*; I ſubmit to your conſideration, whether it would

not

---

* Quintil. Inſt. lib. ii. cap. 12. They always cry loud, and deliver all their diſcourſe in a ſort of extaſy, with a hollow bellowing tone, a frantick action, deep ſighs, furious geſtures, violent toſſing of their arms, and mad-like notions of their heads.—'tis wonderful what effect theſe things have upon the ſurrounding mob; a man of learning ſuits his pronunciation and action to his ſubject, chuſes to be modeſt, and to appear ſo; they call this delivering their diſcourſe with force, tho' it be rather with force.

† 2 Peter ii. 8.

not to be proper to pitch upon the place defigned
for the fcene of the field preaching, at leaft upon
the communion Sunday, at a confiderable diftance
from the church; this would draw off the mob,
the contraft between the folemn action within doors
and the comical fcene without, would be lefs ftrike-
ing; the communicants would breathe a freer air,
they would be lefs diftracted in their devotions,
have eafier accefs to come up to the table or to
return to their feats, and the whole might be tranf-
acted with lefs buftle and confufion, and with more
decency and order. As it is managed at prefent,
it is liker any thing than the adminiftration of the
fupper of our Lord; not a man among us would
be content with a common meal ferved up in fuch
confufion; I am fure that it is impoffible for me,
and I believe it is very difficult for any one, to carry
up with him that fedatenefs of foul, and calmnefs
of thought, that I prefume to think are neceffary,
when he approaches the table of the Lord. How
fhould he? when he is forced to wreftle through
a crowd, to pufh and to be pufhed, ftunned with a
general hubbub, the feats rattling, the galleries
founding, the people finging, the communicants
joftling one another in the crowded paffages, fome
falling, others fainting, and in all corners of the
church, hurry, confufion, and noife. I never fee
our tables * filled up, but it gives me an idea of
the diftraction at Babel when the confufion of
languages began to be felt. I fubmit it, whether
the apoftle's cenfure of the Corinthian church

be

---

* In the kirks in Scotland they have long tables, at which
they fit and communicate; they will hold about an hundred
or more, and when thefe remove to make room for others,
there is the utmoft confufion, as the kirk is crowded with
fpectators, and one part is ftruggling to get from the table
and the other wreftling to get to it.

be not pertinent here, *That is not to eat the Lord's supper*.

PERHAPS the communicants fhould be left a little more to their own meditations, at leaft for my own part I could wifh, that while the elements are handing about, there were obferved (if it be poffible) a folemn and univerfal filence, that we might have time for our private devotions, and an opportunity to afk the bleffing of God upon his word and ordinances; efpecially as it is either forbidden, or become unfafhionable with us, to do fo when we take our feats or finifh the fervice. Thefe Things I have mentioned, and I fubmit my thoughts to the wifdom and candour of the rulers of our church. There ftill remains a very folemn and interefting part of our worfhip, I mean that of public prayer, upon which I beg leave with all fubmiffion to make fome few remarks, earneftly entreating that they may be confidered with calmnefs and impartiality by your reverences, and the other members of our church; and that tho' my fentiments fhould not pleafe, yet in charity you will believe that I wifh well to the proteftant caufe, the intereft of religion, and the purity and peace of the church of Scotland. Thefe, I prefume to think, would be greatly promoted, by the compofition and eftablifhment of fome devout liturgy, or form of prayer, for publick worfhip. Have patience, and hear me out! I was once as much prejudiced againft a propofal of this nature as you can be at prefent, and if you will confider the inconvenience that attends our prefent way of worfhip as calmly as I think I have done, you may perhaps fee the neceffity and advantages of a form of prayer as clearly as I do.

I befeech

* 1 Corinth. ii. 20.

I befeech you then to reflect, that our prefent extemporary way of worfhip is contrary to the practice and opinion of all mankind, in all ages, and of all religions; until it was introduced amidft the ferment and confufion of the fifteenth century; for before that time, whatever was the object of mens worfhip, whatever the matter of their prayers, or however widely they differed in the articles of their creed, yet they agreed as unanimoufly in the ufe of forms of prayer for their publick worfhip, as they did in the belief of a God. Greeks and Romans, the Magi and the Mahometans, Jews and Chriftians, have all agreed in this practice. I have often heard our Mafs John, honeft man, urge the univerfal confent and opinion of mankind, againft the atheifts, as a proof of the exiftence of a Deity; if this argument be conclufive when applied to the firft and greateft article of religion, I mean the exiftence of God, fure it will be fo too, with refpect to the beft and fitteft way of worfhiping him. But what is ftill more, God himfelf prefcribed this way of worfhip to the Jews, as in the cafes of murder, when the perfon who committed it was unknown; of fufpicion of adultery; and when the firft fruits were prefented; his fon our Saviour honoured this way of worfhip with his prefence (for the worfhip of the fynagogues was by a form prayer;) he fanctified it by his practice, for in his agony in the garden, he rofe up, awakened, aud rebuked the difciples, returned to the fame place, repeated the fame form of words three times over; and, before he expired upon the crofs, he offered up his devotions, in the words of the twenty-fecond Pfalm; he authorized it by his command, for our directory for prayer informs us, that our Lord's prayer, is not only a pattern for prayer, but itfelf a moft comprehenfive prayer;

fo that if the command of God himfelf, the example, practice, and command of his Son be fufficient to point out, in what way he would be worfhiped, a form of prayer is pointed out for that purpofe: whereas it cannot be proved that ever God commanded extemporary public prayer; that ever his Son attended worfhip performed in that way; that ever he practifed it, or ever commanded it; nay I am not certain, that there is one example of extemporary publick prayer in all the Bible, at leaft I am fure there is not an Inftance that will correfpond with our fituation, or authorife us in the ufe of it, when fo many and fo great inconveniencies do attend it.

WE complain, and very juftly too, that the popifh clergy are too affuming, and claim a fuperiority over the laity, inconfiftent with the natural rights of mankind, and the relation of brethren formed by the covenant of grace; pardon me, gentlemen, if I fay that you claim a very extraordinary fuperiority over the laity, in the cafe before us; every one of you claims an exclufive privilege of manufacturing our publick prayers, and affumes a right of making us fay to the Deity, whatever he thinks fit. In the moft momentous affair in which we can be concerned upon earth, we muft depend entirely upon the difcretion, honefty, and ability of every private parfon, and take the words and matter of our addreffes to our God and Maker, fuch as he is pleafed to give, without ever feeing, examining, or judging for ourfelves. This is really treating us as if we were children or fools; we allow that you have a right to offer our prayers; and is it not fit that we fhould all fpeak, the minifter may be called the mouth of the congregation; but the mouth of the congrregation fhould fpeak the mind of the congregation. In

our

our congregations the mouth runs before the mind, and speaks without giving us any opportunity of thinking what we ought to speak, and often says things that we should certainly reject, and sometimes offers petitions that we should absolutely abhor, had we time calmly to examine them: our mouth leads us into the gross blunder of presenting our addresses to the Deity first, and next judging whether they be proper addresses after they are offered, when we cannot mend what is wrong, or alter, what is improper; we absurdly begin where we should end; for, in the natural order of things, the congregation should first be satisfied that the prayers are proper to be offered, and then the minister should offer them in their name; just as a prudent man will think before he speaks; but in our *admirable* plan of worship the congregation speaks by its mouth, before it has considered what it is to say; that is, the parson offers up the petition, and the people may judge of its propriety after it is offered, if they please.

THE absurdity here is so glaring, that it is astonishing that it escapes the observation of the laity; and it would not escape them in any other instance. Should the ablest member in the house of commons, propose to offer an address to his majesty, in the name of the house, without communicating it to the members, the impropriety would be immediately perceived. When the estates, or counties, design to address their sovereign, offer your service, and tell them, " Pray gentlemen give yourselves no trouble about the matter, we and our brethren will each of us address the King in our own way; trust the whole affair to us, every individual of the cloth is more than sufficient for the undertaking; it is your business to approve of whatever we are pleased to say for you;

or

or at leaſt, you may conſider how you like the addreſs, after it hath been offered." Take this advice, and try if the laity will be as compliſant with reſpect to the honour of their prince, and the concerns of their bodies, as they are with reſpect to the honour of their God and the intereſts of their ſouls ; yet one would be tempted to think (if the common conſent of this nation were not againſt the opinion) that the laity are as much intereſted in an addreſs to the Deity, as in one to the King ; and that they would be at leaſt as loath to truſt the firſt, as the laſt, to the diſcretion, ability, or honeſty of every man who chanced to put on a black coat or wear a ſtarched band. But the groſſeſt abſurdity will be ſwallowed down when it is in faſhion, and I think there can hardly be a groſſer one, than that a gentleman ſhould mount the pulpit, of whoſe principles or diſcretion we have no knowledge at all, and that this man ſhould have a right to dictate the prayers of a whole congregation. If we will believe the author of the Characteriſtics *, who ſeems to ſpeak from experience, there are among you many whoſe principles are very dangerous and very inconſiſtent with the religion of Jeſus ; yet theſe men not only lead, but even compoſe the devotions of the people, and make us poor lay men addreſs our Maker upon any principles that they pleaſe.

I have come from my houſe a ſound orthodox chriſtian, and have hardly taken my ſeat in the church, when I have found myſelf praying, or at leaſt one was praying in my name, as a rank Socinian. I have been made an Arrian as to my prayers very often ; and in ſhort, there has hardly any whimſical opinion been broached among the

clergy

---

* Eccleſiaſtical Characteriſtics, publiſhed at Glaſgow 1756.

clergy for thefe forty years, that I have not fome-
time or other found mixed with my public prayers,
tho' for my part I am a plain old fafhioned man,
and content myfelf with the apoftles creed.   Sometimes, indeed, for my heart I could not have told
upon what particular principles my prayers were
offered, they were fo *excellently well contrived, and fo
free from all narrow notions*, that they would have
ferved a Jewifh fynagogue, a Mahometan mofque,
or a congregation of Perfian magi, as well or better
than a Chriftian affembly.   If the minifter that
officiates be a fceptic, I am made to pray like a fceptic ; if an enthufiaft, he addreffes God in my name,
according to his own enthufiaftical notions ; when
he chances to be a fractious firebrand, or a keen party man, tho' I be a very peaceable tradefman, my
prayers breathe faction, my devotions in public
are flaming with party heat, and tinctured with
the fury of his faction.   It is well known, that
when any difputes happen, and differences arife
among the clergy in their fynods or affemblies, both
fides appeal to Heaven in their public prayers, and
force the laity to appeal with them (we are not fup-
pofed to have any right to judge for ourfelves in
thefe cafes ;) and what is even worfe, by an unlucky
change of minifters, or by ftepping into another
church, I have often been made to appeal to heaven
as an advocate for both fides of the queftion, and
pray for and againft each of the parties in one day :
for tho' our churches have the appearance of the
fame worfhip, they are as different as the tempers,
principles, and parties of the parfons who manufacture it ; and this leads the laity into the dangerous
blunder of offering contradictory petitions, and praying at different times, upon principles as oppofite to
one another, as light is to darknefs. It is an ufual thing
                                                        amongft

àmongſt us to pray for and againſt preſentations in one week; I have thanked God for his decrees of election and reprobation in the forenoon, and in the afternoon offered my humble thanks that all men have equal acceſs to ſalvation, by faith and virtue. In a word, there is no party, nor different principle among our clergy, with reſpect to which I have not been made to play faſt and looſe with the Deity, to aſk what I did not want, and to pray againſt what I moſt earneſtly wiſhed for. This we call worſhiping God! but did we deal ſo with our fellow men, they would call it mockery, and take it as a groſs affront: I cannot help thinking, gentlemen, that this will appear, even to yourſelves, hard treatment of the laity, and that you will acknowledge, that their judgment ought not to be ſo entirely made a property of, as to oblige them to have their publick worſhip offered upon what principles the parſon pleaſes to eſpouſe; or upon opoſite principles, as the miniſter for the time is of this or the other party. One of your cloth complains that we betray * viſible impatience till prayer be over; is it any wonder if we do? for as it is managed at preſent, prayer is to us a very dangerous part of worſhip; for as that judicious gentleman obſerves, *A great deal more, a vaſt deal more, depends upon our performance of this duty with judgment and propriety, than moſt people ſeem to be aware of.* They who are aware of this, cannot help being impatient and uneaſy, when a duty of ſuch vaſt importance is truſted to every individual of the clergy; and they who ſeldom think of its nature or importance will always eſteem it a dry and lifeleſs part of our ſervice.

* Mr. Fordice's Edification by publick Inſtitutions.

I am

I am apt to think, that it is fometimes happy for our laity that they only hear prayer as they do fermons, and cannot, I believe, as it is at prefent performed, or leaft I am fure do not join in it, for tho' it be criminal not to worfhip God in public, yet it feems to be as great if not a greater crime to offer an irrational worfhip, to infult him with contradictory petitions with minifters of oppofite parties, and to have our devotions tinctured with the fpirit of faction, the wild dreams of enthufiafts, the dangerous notions of fceptics, and the abfurd follies of men whofe heads are filled with vapours and whims. Tho' thefe fhould fometimes be mixed with your difcourfes, the hardfhip and danger would not be half fo great. If they did inftruct, they might amufe; and we needed not embrace your notions unlefs we pleafed; our own reafon might expel the poifon. But when they are wrought into our publick prayers, there remains no remedy; we muft take thefe as you are pleafed to give them, or go away without public worfhip.

The popifh clergy indeed put a great hardfhip uuon the laity, by offering their prayers in an unknown tongue; but tho' the hardfhip be great, it admits of fome remedies; they may have their prayers tranflated into their refpective languages; they may have them explained by thofe that underftand the language; and conftant ufe of the fame forms, may in time enable them to annex proper ideas to the words: but the hardfhip put upon us admits of no remedy; we muft offer what prayers every clergyman pleafes, we muft underftand them the beft way we can, we muft pick up the words as we can catch them, according to the ftrength of your voices, the diftinctnefs of your pronunciation, and the largenefs of the church; the fall

of

of a Bible, the opening of a feat, or a cough in any corner of the church, will lofe us half a fentence; and yet if we would pray with the underftanding, we muft collect the feveral parts of the fentence, fupply the words that are loft, compare it with what went before, examine, approve, and offer it; and this muft be all done in a breath. I queftion whether the parfon could perform this tafk himfelf; and I am convinced that it is impoffible for the flow and ignorant part of the audience; efpecially as fome of you fpeak fo faft, that we cannot keep pace with you barely in hearing what you fay; others deliver fo flowly, that our memories cannot ferve us to collect the feveral parts of the fentence; fome are fo fond of new and learned words, that one half of the congregation cannot know their meaning; and many of you have fuch a perplexed, intricate way of expreffing yourfelves, that we find it impoffible to difcover the import of your petitions; and perhaps would find this a difficult tafk, tho' we had an opportunity to confider them at leifure in our clofets.

So that putting all thefe difficulties together, I imagine that it will appear that the laity of the kirk of Scotland lie under greater hardfhips, with refpect to public worfhip, than the laity of any church upon earth; and this hardfhip is made ftill more galling to thofe who have fenfe enough to feel it, by the pompous harangues that we are frequently entertained with, upon the privileges that we poffefs above other chriftians, the religious liberty we enjoy, and the fingular purity of our worfhip. Sure, gentlemen, you muft mean *yourfelves*, when you afcribe thefe great bleffings to our church, or you infult us in the more cruel manner; if you mean that you enjoy great privileges, and a moft extenfive liberty, it is very true; for you

pray

pray what you pleaſe, you ſing what you pleaſe, you teach what you pleaſe, and our whole public worſhip is ſo much of your own manufacturing that there can hardly be found room for a verſe or two of ſcripture, and theſe you chuſe as you pleaſe; in a word, every pariſh miniſter is a little pope, ſubject to none but a general council, and, like the great pope, not ſubject to that, but when he pleaſes: for it ſeems to be a point as much diſputed in the preſbyterian church, whether a miniſter is obliged to ſubmit to the ſentence of a general aſſembly, as it is in the popiſh, whether his holineſs ought to yield obedience to a general council. So that it muſt be acknowledged, that you enjoy a great many privileges, and a moſt extenſive liberty. But pray what privileges, do we enjoy, when one man's judgment preſcribes to a whole pariſh? when we muſt pray for or againſt whatever party the parſon pleaſes? offer our devotions according to the religious or political principles that the miniſter for the time chuſes to embrace? ſhift ſides as your humours change, and addreſs our God, as Arrians, Socinians, or Sceptics, as the gentleman in the pulpit is inclined?——Sure, if our civil liberty were not ſomething more ſubſtantial, we ſhould be the greateſt ſlaves in Europe!—Again, what purity can there poſſibly be in our worſhip, when the paſſions, prejudices, and whimſical opinions of every miniſter may, and do mix with it? I have always been at a loſs to determine whether your confidence in entertaining us with ſuch harangues, and your power of face in keeping your countenances, ſtifling the laugh, or our ſtupidity in not perceiving the groſs affront, and patience in not reſenting it, were moſt to be admired. I cannot imagine you are ſo weak as to think with the bulk of our people, that our worſhip muſt of conſe-

quence

quence be pure, if it be different from the practice of the church of Rome ; and that we can only err upon the fide of fuperftition. If this be your opinion, it refembles the conduct of fome germans, of whom I have read, who, for fear of the roman army, ran into a river and were drowned. Juft fo the greateft part of our people (for I believe better things of you) conclude that our worfhip muft be pure, if we do not worfhip images, pray to faints, or adore the virgin Mary, tho' it be mixed with the whimfical notions, enthufiaftic opinions, and filly noftrums of every quack doctor in divinity. It would be happy if you would content yourfelves, with infulting the people only, with fuch harangues ; but you often make them infult their God, or at leaft, you do it in their names, by thanking him for eftablifhing a pure worfhip which he did not eftablifh ; a work which cannot poffibly be pure ; and which even in our own opinion is not pure ; for if the moderate party confifts of fuch minifters as the author of the Characteriftics * (who is faid to be one of your or-der) has reprefented them to the world, God have mercy upon the fouls committed to their care! and may the Almighty pity and relieve the congregations whofe devotions they compofe, dictate, and offer. Yet in all probability if the moderate men were to write Characteriftics, they would give us as for-bidding a picture of the party that our author is pleafed to call orthodox. What then muft become of us poor lay men, whofe fouls were bandied about between the factions, and our prayers offered fome-times upon the principles of the one, and fome-times upon the principles of the other ? would it not be happy for us, that we had fome pious,

* Ecclefiaftical Characteriftics, publifhed at Glafgow 1756.

primi-

primitive form of prayer, that would fecure the purity and reafonablenefs of our prayers, let the minifters private opinions be what they would? As things are at prefent, it is impoffible that our fervice can either be reafonable, perfect, or pure; unlefs we can fuppofe, that our church has a privilege, which no church upon earth ever had or ever claimed; I mean, that no weak or whimfical minifter, no factious fire-brand, no fceptic or enthufiaft can mount our pulpits; or that after men of thefe characters get into them, they will pray better than they are able, upon principles that they do not believe, or with a calmnefs which they do not poffefs. Now fuppofing, that there are only an * hundred of our minifters of fome or other of the above characters, and that one with another each of them has 500 fouls under his charge, there will be 50,000 perfons in Scotland, who never worfhip God in public in the way of his own appointment, and whofe public worfhip muft be dangerous to themfelves, and unacceptable to the deity. Where muft the blood of thefe poor people fall, but upon the rulers of our church? who, tho' they have found by fatal experience, that all the fubfcriptions in the world will not hinder men of pernicious principles from creeping into the church, yet will not take the only effectual method to prevent them from doing mifchief there.

But befides the injuftice of affuming to yourfelves a right to dictate to us what prayers you pleafe; befides the abfurdity of making us offer contradictory petitions, and leaving our public

---

* This is not an unreafonable calculation in thefe latter ages, confidering, that there was one of twelve who proved a traitor, even when our lord was vifibly prefent with our church.

worfhip

worſhip expoſed to the whims and follies of the ſcep-
tic and enthuſiaſt, there are many other inconve-
niences that attend our preſent method. Firſt, it is
a queſtion whether the laity can join at all in our
public prayers; for we muſt either ſuppoſe that
they go along with the miniſter, offering every
word as he utters it, or wait until he has finiſhed
the ſentence, and then examine it, and give their
aſſent. If the firſt be their method, it is evident
that they place an abſurd and dangerous confidence
in the honeſty and ability of the parſon, and embrace in their prayers all the whimſical notions and
pernicious principles that he may chance to mix
with them: and further, that many of them, will,
like parrots, talk what they do not underſtand, ſince
many words will occur, whoſe meaning and importance they are not able all at once to conceive.
At leaſt I find it ſo with myſelf. Perhaps our people
may be inſpired with more than ordinary penetration
in the time of prayer; but, at other times, I find it
difficult enough to make many of them comprehend
an ordinary meſſage, delivered in the plaineſt words
that I can poſſibly find; and after repeating it over
and over again, have the mortification to find, that
they miſunderſtand me, tho' the whole paſſage does
not exceed two ſentences. That theſe men ſhould underſtand all the expreſſions in an extemporary prayer,
and with their underſtandings and judgments keep
pace with the miniſter for half an hour, or twenty
minutes, to me appears impoſſible, and I believe,
will appear even to you very miraculous. But ſuppoſe that our people wait till the miniſter has finiſhed the ſentence, and then compare the ſeveral
parts, examine the whole, and give their aſſent,
God knows how unfit maay of them are for this
taſk; but let them be ever ſo fit, if a word be loſt,
if one occurs whoſe meaning they do not under-

ſtand,

ſtand, or if the arrangement of the words be perplexed, it is evident that they cannot give a rational aſſent: and if they take time to examine what
may be ſuſpicious, to ſupply what is loſt, or to unravel what is perplexed, let them be as quick as they
will, the ſubſequent ſentence will be loſt.   I do not
indeed ſuppoſe that the bulk of our congregations
ever dreamt of theſe difficulties, becauſe they give
themſelves no trouble about underſtanding, examining, or aſſenting; but content themſelves with
being humble hearers, and perhaps in all their lives
never once gave a ſincere and rational Amen to
publick prayers; though hearing another pray, and
joining in prayer, be very different things.

Another inconvenience that attends our way of
worſhip is, that young gentlemen, juſt come from
the univerſity, full fraught with philoſophy, and
fond of ſhewing their learning, very injudiciouſly
vent their notions in our public prayers.   A young
ſpruce gentleman the other Sunday converted us in
an inſtant, from plain country people, into profound
philoſophers, and theſe too of the dogmatical kind;
for we told God Almighty many things concerning
his own works, which the learned gentleman, it
ſeems, thought he did not know before, many things
that we neither underſtood nor believed; we travelled
ſo high, that our heads began to turn, and after
all loſt our gentleman, for fifteen minutes, amongſt
things that he called vortices, and began indeed to
ſuſpect that he was ſwallowed up by them, or had
gone where Milton tells us all vain and empty things
go,

Up whirl'd aloft,
Fly o'er the backſide of the world far off.
Into a limbo large and broad, ſince call'd
The paradiſe of fools †.

† Milt. Parad. Loſt, book iii. 495.

C   Whether

Whether he vifited that place or not we cannot tell, but we found him at laſt upon earth, chafing a mole. Had he been pleaſed to tell us theſe things, ſtripped of their philofophic garb, in a ſermon, ſome of them might have been entertaining, ſome of them uſeful, and moſt of them tolerable; but to make us inform the Deity of things that we nei‐ ther knew nor believed, and as it were inſtruct our Maker in the nature, beauty, and order of his own works, (I humbly think) was imprudent and pre‐ ſumptuous. However, he made a ſhift, by new coined words, and terms of art, to be far above the reach of our underſtandings; and to pray with him, we muſt have read Euclid, ſtudied Newton's works more than our Bibles, and brought half a dozen dictionaries to church with us, to help us to the meaning of his words. The gentleman how‐ ever obtained his end, the people ſtared, and, when they came out, concluded that he was ad‐ mirably learned, and that none was fo fit to be their miniſter. Upon this whim, they vigorouſly op‐ poſe the ſettlement of a pious and prudent gentle‐ man, prefented to the charge by the patron, and are moſt piouſly ſupported in their wiſe oppoſition by a ſet of the clergy, I ſuppoſe for conſcience ſake. But I beg pardon, digreſſion is a fault. My bu‐ ſineſs is only with our public worſhip; and I flatter myſelf that you will own, that upon that Sunday it was but poorly performed: yet ſuch farces as theſe we are often forced to bear with; and inſtead of the humble expreſſions of penitents, the conciſe peti‐ tions of poor mortals, and the grateful thankſgiv‐ ings of rational creatures, to their merciful God, our prayers frequently conſiſt of the fooliſh oſten‐ tation of learning, and the harſh jargon of hard words.

NEITHER

NEITHER does our worſhip ſuffer more by the oſtentatious folly and pedantic humour of our young dominies, than by the natural and necef-ſary decays of the invention, memory and judg-ment of our aged miniſters; for as the clergy are fooliſh enough to vie in the expences of dreſs, table, and equipage, with the landed gentlemen, moſt of them are unable, and all of them are unwilling to call an aſſiſtant, as long as they are able to creep up to a pulpit, and prattle out ſomething like a prayer; ſo that you will frequently find a man inventing and dictating the devotions of a congregation, who is ſuperannuated to all the other affairs of life. This man it ſeems has a right to make us addreſs our Maker, in what manner, and with what words he thinks proper; tho' in common converſation, we cannot help perceiving that his memory has loſt its ſtrength, that his under-ſtanding is decayed; and all the powers of his mind are ſadly declined. It would perhaps be cruel, to give inſtances of the blunders, blaſphemy, and nonſenſe that have been mixed with our prayers by this misfortune, tho' many inſtances might be produced; but it is (I humbly think) more cruel and highly unreaſonable, to put the aged miniſters under the neceſſity of expoſing their weakneſs, and diſhonouring the ſervice of their Maker; and the laity under the hardſhip, either of offering nonſenſe, or blaſphemy, inſtead of pious ardent, and expreſſive prayers, or of reducing their miniſter, to want and beggary in his old age, by forcing him to call an aſſiſtant whether he can maintain him or not; eſpecially, as all danger might be prevented, and all deficiencies ſupplied, by compoſing and eſtabliſhing a pious form of prayer; for he might read a prayer very devoutly, and diſtinctly, when he cannot invent readily, or

         dictate

dictate an extemporary prayer to the congregation with
propriety and judgment ; or if he chanced to blunder, or pronounce inftinctly, having the form before us, we could eafily fupply the defects ; we
could much better put up with trifling in his fermons,
and patiently hear him prattle about his fubject and
about it, becaufe we could fupply our lofs, in fome
meafure, by reading fome of the beft fermons ourfelves, or to our families ; but public prayer is a
matter of that importance, that there is no poffibility of fupplying it by our own induftry, no rectify-
ing miftakes after the prayer is offered, and no poffibility of preventing very grofs and dangerous blunders, while we perform this part of our worfhip
after the prefent method : for tho' our aged minifters
fhould retain all the powers of their minds to the
laft, which is not the cafe with one in an hundred';
tho' they fhould be able to invent extemporary
petitions, with propriety ; yet as the organs of
the body decay, it is impoffible that they can
exprefs them with that ftrength of voice, and
diftinctnefs of pronunciation, which are neceffary
to us, before we can give a very rational affent,
if we can at all give a rational affent to prayers that
we never have examined ; no, nor yet the minifter
himfelf. The weak voice, the trembling body,
the want of teeth, and other infirmities incident to
old age, do often render the pronunciation fo indif-
tinct, that in our prefent way of worfhip one half of
the congregation is at as great a lofs, as if the gentleman prayed in an unknown tongue ; or at moft they
can only pick up a word here and there, without any
connexion.   Let us fuppofe that among more than
a thoufand minifters, there are only eighty whofe
underftandings, or bodily organs, are thus decayed, and that, one with another, each of them

has

has five-hundred fouls under his charge; it would be a misfortune to thofe who are under the care of the firft, if they did join in the public worfhip as it is performed amongft them; and they who are under the care of the laft cannot poffibly do it; fo that there muft be in Scotland at leaft forty-thoufand perfons, who are debarred from the moft effential part of public worfhip, by the old age of our minif-ters, joined with the abfurdity of our prefent plan; to which if we add the 50,000 I mentioned before, there will be ninety thoufand perfons in this nation who cannot worfhip God at all in public, or worfhip him a way unworthy of him, and dangerous to them-felves, whofe blood muft be crying to heaven a-gainft the rulers of our church. For whether the above calculations be allowed to be juft or not, there muft certainly be a very confiderable number of our brethren in this diftreffed fituation; unlefs we fup-pofe, contrary to known matter of fact, that the mi-nifters of our church are not yet fubjected to the fame infirmities of body and mind that other men are fubject to; and that they are fecured, by fome fa-cred infallibility, from embracing enthufiaftical or fceptical opinions.

But further, our worfhip as it is performed at prefent, is not only corrupted by the contrary petitions of contending parties; not only tinctured with the heats and animofities that arife in fynods and affemblies; not only mixed with the whimfical opinions, and pernicious principles of libertines and enthufiafts, that climb up into our pulpits; not only rendered obfcure and contemptible by the pedantry and affected learning of the younger, and the weakneffes of mind and body of our older minifters; but frequently interlaid with ill-timed compliments to the great, or the minifter's fa-

vourites

vourites, and the groffeft abufes of thofe who have the misfortune to be out of favour. I could produce numerous inftances of both, and, were it not an inviduous tafk, point out the perfons, places, and times. Upon the marriage of a certain noble peer in this nation, the parfon carried his compliments fo far in the public prayers, that he exceeded all the bounds of decency, and made his female hearers blufh ; and I would blufh to repeat to the rulers of our church in a letter the expreffions that he made ufe of to the God of heaven and earth in the face of a congregation ; fo extravagant and ill chofen were his words, that the lady was forced to direct the clergyman, and intreat him to forbear his rude petitions. A minifter, even in one of our royal burghs, obferving a young gentleman, fon to one of the magiftrates, in church, after a journey to London, made all the congregation thank God that he had brought back their friends from foreign lands. Moft men, I prefume, will remember how grofsly the royal commander of his majefty's forces, during the laft war, was abufed by having his praifes wrought into our public prayers, by rough and unfkilful hands ; fome allowances, I own, are to be made for the clergy in this inftance ; the augmentation fcheme was then in agitation, and the weaker part of them foolifhly thought, that this would pave the way for it.

On the other hand, he muft be a great ftranger in our congregations, or very heedlefs when he comes there, who has not obferved that fometimes a well meant zeal, and fometimes too warm an attachment to party opinions with refpect to religious fubjects, and private refentments too, have taught minifters of keen paffions, to ufe feveral expreffions, not only inconfiftent with the charity

of

of chriftians, but even with the humanity of men; *Vex them in thy wrath, and plead with them in thy difpleafure through all eternity*, was the unchriftian petition of Mr.——with a refpect to papifts; *Pour down the vials of thy wrath upon them, and burn their flefh with fire*, was Mr. C—'s ungenerous wifh. Nothing but heat of zeal and hurry of paffion could have dictated thefe petitions; and I am far from thinking that many of our minifters fuffer themfelves to be driven to fo great lengths. But all of them are fubject to paffions, and what is left to the difcretion of the minifter, is left alfo to the indifcretion and paffions of the man; and we frequently find the two laft, where the firft was defigned to take place. Many inftances could be given of the ill-timed flattery of friends, and unchriftian expreffions with refpect to enemies, that have been vented in our public prayers; but I am tender of the reputation of the clergy, and do not chufe to expofe their errors, farther than is abfolutely neceffary to fhew the danger and abfurdity of our prefent way of worfhip; and to perfuade them to recover and fecure its purity and decency; and therefore, I humbly intreat you to confider, whether the ill-timed, ill-chofen compliments of fycophants upon the one hand, and the unchriftian expreffions of keen zealots upon the other, do not render our public worfhip contemptible and dangerous; and whether there be any thing fo likely to prevent them from indulging their humours, to the difhonour of God and difgrace of religion, as fome well-chofen, pious, public form of prayer.

AFTER flattery we may mention politics, in which our minifters will be dabbling, in fpite of grace, nature, and common fenfe, as another very fruitful fource of blunders in our public worfhip,

few

few of them have genius, fewer ftill have fufficient intelligence, and all of them are at too great a diftance from the feat of government, or to comprehend the fecret intrigues of courts, or to perceive, in fpite of the varnifh by which they are difguifed, the real views of parties ; yet all of them will be meddling, and in every difpute our prayers muft take a fide, and the poor lay-men muft addrefs their Maker, fometimes upon the faith of a foolifh rumour, and often upon the credit of a common news. To fay nothing of the times very wittily but very truly defcribed by Butler in his Hudibras,

When gofpel trumpeter, furrounded
With long-ear'd rout, to battle founded
And pulpit, drum ecclefiaftic,
Was beat by fift inftead of a ftick

Not (I fay) to mention thefe days, whofe hiftory will be an eternal difgrace to our religion, and would furnifh as many inftances of nonfenfe and blafphemy vented in our public prayers, as would be fufficient to fill up a large volume; even in latter days, politics have introduced very grofs abfurdities, into our public fervice. I am not yet an old man, and I remember to have been made to pray, that God would pull down *the bloody houfe of Auftria:* during the laft war, I earneftly begged that he would build it up; now I begin to give broad hints that I would have it pulled down again; and am expecting every Sunday, to be made to defire it, in a formal manner. The Interefts and leagues of the ftates of Europe fhift fo frequently, that we are often flung out in our prayers, and pray for our enemies as if they were our friends, and againft our friends as if they were enemies. Would our minifters be
contented

contented to make us pray in general for our friends, and againſt the devices of our enemies, we ſhould never be wrong: but they chuſe to mention whom they meaṅ, leſt omniſcient wiſdom ſhould miſtake, or at leaſt that their people may know that they are great politicians, and very zealous for the public good. Many a time have I thanked God for giving us glorious victories, when we have been ſhamefully beat; for inſpiring courage into our troops, when they have run away; for ſuccefs granted to our arms in battles that were never fought; and for deliverances from plots that were never formed. Our public worſhip, in the preſent way, has always been and will always be tinctured with the ſpirit of party, and made the property of faction in church and ſtate. When the famous Cambuſlang's converſion was going on (I ſhall never forget it), one Sunday morning I was made to thank Goa for the manifeſtation of his power in that converſion, and intreat him to continue the great work he had begun; in the afternoon, by an unlucky change of miniſters, I was made to pray that God would put a ſtop to the deluſions of the devil, by which the ignorant and ſimple were deceived, and give us grace to reſiſt that ſpirit of enthuſiaſm that had gone out into our land: thus what I aſcribed to God in the morning, I aſcribed to the Devil in the afternoon; and what I had requeſted God to promote, I requeſted him too to give me grace to reſiſt. I prayed long and earneſtly with Walpole's enemies, before their intrigues and my prayers could pull him down; and when he fell, I was made to thank God for the great deliverance; though it was ſoon diſcovered, that it was nothing more than a ſtruggle for power between parties, and a matter of no moment to me or my country which of the parties was in or out: however, all ranks contri-

buted

buted fomething to raife the clamour; the mob made bonfires, the magiftrates rung bells, the minifters gave their prayers, and the mountain brought forth a moufe.

Nay, I have known the private piques and little quarrels between the parfon and his neighbours, introduced into our public worfhip and made a part of our prayers: even when the parfon was the firft aggreffor, he had the affurance to complain to God (as he called it), and what was ftill more unreafonable, made his parifhoners complain with him, or at leaft, he complained in their names, though moft of them were very fenfible, that he himfelf had done the injuftice; how his complaints were received in heaven I cannot tell, but I know that they had their effects upon earth, for his antagonift, unable to bear the ftaring of the congregation every Lord's-day, was forced to fit down under the injuftice. It is hard to determine in this refpect, whether you have the meaneft opinion of your God or your hearers; for it feems you think that both are obliged to fhift fides as you are pleafed to direct them, and, right or wrong, be ftill of the party which the parfon for the time thinks fit to embrace. That you fhould treat the laity with fo great contempt in this cafe, is not fo furprizing, as you may be convinced from long experience, that they will fwallow down the groffeft abfurdities in their public prayers, and truft the propriety of their worfhip upon Sunday, to the difcretion and ability of a man, whofe folly and weaknefs perhaps they laugh at all the week. But I own it is amazing that you can ufe fuch freedom with the Deity, to defire him to do and undo as the fancy ftrikes you, or your defigns chance to alter.

Our prayers are, for the moft part, too hiftorical and feem rather defigned to inftruct the congregation,

gregation, than to confefs their fins, exprefs their wants, or offer their grateful thankfgivings. I do not at all fuppofe that you are ignorant, as our people feem to be, of the difference between preaching and praying, or that you are not fenfible that a very good fermon, will make but a very bad prayer ; but I cannot help thinking that you comply too far with the popular tafte in this refpect, and ftrive to pleafe, by giving our public prayers as much the air and manner of a fermon as poffible ; or knowing that many of your people judge of the propriety and excellency of a prayer by its length, to come up to the common ftandard you are forced to fill up a gap with what materials come firft to hand ; and this I am more apt to believe to be the cafe, becaufe we fometimes find half a dozen of fentences from fcripture poured into our prayers all at once, without the leaft connexion among themfelves, or the leaft relation to what went before, or follows after ; and frequently too, without the leaft affinity to any of the parts of prayer. What Mr. Fordyce means, by that certain * happy irregularity in our public prayer, which he is pleafed to recommend, I profefs I know not; but I know very well, that there is a certain unhappy irregularity in moft of ours, that renders them very improper for public worfhip. The feveral parts of prayer are moft abfurdly confounded, though they require very different difpofitions of heart ; confeffion is jumbled with thankfgiving ; petition is mixed with narration ; and fometimes we have all the parts of prayer in one fingle fentence. By thefe means the mind is held in fufpence, and cannot fettle to that humility, conviction, and forrow, that ought to attend confeffion ; nor is it raifed to that

---

* Edification, &c. page 15.

warm gratitude, and ardent love, that ought to enliven our thankfgivings; neither is it filled with
that fenfe of dependence, nor formed to that ferious
earneftnefs and lively faith, with which our petitions
ought to be fent forth.

INSTEAD of thefe, amufed with the novelty of
expreffion, and diftracted with the quick and irre-
gular fucceffions of the feveral parts of prayer, it
fluctuates between thefe fenfations, and feels not
much of any of them. When all the powers of
the foul fhould be employed in their proper places,
and making their greateft efforts to offer a fpiritual
worfhip to the Father of fpirits, our curiofity is
only awake, and we are liftening to a prayer no
otherways than we do to a fermon. I would beg
leave further to obferve, that our extemporary worfhip in the church, produces very bad effects with
repect to our worfhip in our families; for as praying to God extempore is the prevailing fafhion,
and as our people are taught to defpife worfhip offered by a form, fo thofe of them who want memory, learning, and invention, to exprefs themfelves
extempore with propriety, and have modefty to be
afhamed of indecent expreffions, and reflection to
think of the danger of unreafonable and unchriftian petitions, never pray with their families at all.
On the other hand, when ignorance and felf-fuffi-
ciency meet in the mafter of a family, their worfhip of confequence is a miferable mixture of nonfenfe, error, and blafphemy. The moft ignorant
are always the moft prefuming, and the lefs fenfe
that a man has of the nature and importance of
prayer, the more readily will he venture upon extemporary worfhip. In fact it is true, that many
of our people who can hardly repeat their creed,
and know very little more of their religion than
a few hard words that they have gleaned out of our
                                        catechifms,

catechifms, imitate our parfons in praying extempore; and approach their Maker with as great familiarity, as they would do to their neighbours, and with much lefs refpect and reverence than they dare treat their laird. Good God! what pityful fcenes have I feen of this kind! what rude and fhocking expreffions, what blafphemous petitions have I heard! how often have I trembled when the ignorant and proud enthufiaft kneeled down with his family to his extemporary worfhip! how often have I fhuddered at the whimfical notions that he wrought into our prayers, the infolent and unchriftian expreffions which he ufed, and the nonfenfe that he offered in our name. How often has my heart bled in fecret for the fad fituation of many miferable families, who, by our unhappy attachment to extemporary prayer, either want family-worfhip altogether, or offer their worfhip in fuch a manner as difhonours God, difgraces religion, and is very dangerous to themfelves! but I would very far exceed the bounds of a letter, and I am afraid wearyout your patience, if I fhould endeavour to lay before you all the inconveniencies that attend our prefent way of worfhip; and I flatter myfelf, if you will add to thefe already taken notice of, the blunders of ignorance, the flights of vanity, the needlefs filly repetitions, the unguarded expreffions, and the childifh thoughts that are mixed, with our prayers (and muft be mixed with them, unlefs you can fuppofe that all our minifters are men of the greateft abilities, elocution, and prudence) you will fee, that our prefent way of worfhip is defective, unreafonable, and dangerous; and that the hardfhips that the laity labour under, and the danger to which they are expofed, can only be removed by fome devout and approved form of prayer.

To

To support the present absurd practice, to make the laity sit quietly down with the injustice done them, and to blind their eyes that they may not perceive the disadvantages that they labour under, and the danger to which they are exposed, it has been said that a form of prayer will limit the inspiration of the Spirit; that it deadens the devotion of people; that all the wants of a christian congregation cannot be expressed by a form : and some have been so foolish as to say, that it is unlawful to worship by a form of prayer. Will you pardon my presumption, and hear me with patience, if I humbly offer my thoughts upon these heads; I hope you will. As to the first, I might boldly appeal to your own consciences, and ask you, *In the name of God Do you believe that you are inspired? Have you indeed so mean an opinion of the understanding and judgment of the laity, as to imagine that any of them, who think at all, can ever be brought to believe, that the prayers we commonly hear are dictated by the Holy Ghost? Or have you so little regard to the honour of God and the interests of religion, as to ascribe your extemporary effusions to the Holy Spirit?* No, I am persuaded that none but the rankest enthusiasts will ever urge this argument against a form of prayer; and I will beg leave to ask such, are the words or the matter of your prayers, or both, inspired? That the words are not inspired, is evident from the difficulty that you frequently have to find proper words; from the improper and sometimes indecent expressions that fall from you; from the ill-timed pauses that you are forced to make, and that most useful supplement of coughing, groaning, and spitting, that must come in to your assistance. But supposing that you were indeed inspired with words, it would be of small importance to yourselves or to us, unless the matter of your prayers be be infpired too: and if the matter of them be infpired, your prayers are of equal authority with the fcriptures themfelves, and fhould be entered into the cannon. I know not how to excufe the negligence of the people of this nation, in fuffering fo much found doctrine to be loft; it might have cleared up fome difficult paffages in fcripture, and decided feveral important difputes. I know not what to fay for this piece of negligence, unlefs our people think that all things neceffary for chriftians to know, to believe, and to practife, are revailed in the holy fcriptures; and that they may be taught by them what to afk in prayer, and how to regulate their lives; and if this be true, your infpiration is a very great gift beftowed for very poor purpofes, only to fave you the pains of fearching the fcriptures, and the trouble of compofing a form of prayer by the inftructions and examples contained in them. The heathen poets themfelves had a greater reverence for the Deity than this, for it was a maxim among them

Nec deus interfit, nifi dignus vindice nodus
Inciderit——— *

I fubmit, whether you do not tranfgrefs againft this rule, by introducing the infpiration of the Holy Spirit, if the fcriptures be fufficient to direct us what to afk in prayer; and if they be not fufficient for this, the revelation of the will of God for our falvation is defective in a very important point; and neither the prophets, nor the apoftles, no nor our Saviour himfelf, though he enterprized it, have taught us how to pray. But fuppofing that it were neceffary, that the words and matter of our prayers

* Hor. Art. Poet. Never let a god be introduced, unlefs there happens to be fome difficulty worthy of fuch an agent.

fhould

should be inspired by the Holy Ghost ; why might
not a number of pious and learned divines, met together with such an interesting and great design as
that of composing a form of prayer for a whole
church, have as much reason to expect, and be as
likely to receive the assistance of the Holy Spirit,
as a private clergyman inventing the transient
prayer of a particular congregation ? But this sup-
posed inspiration in our extemporary way, will in-
volve us in very great, nay insuperable difficulties ?
for we shall be as much puzzled where to find our
miraculous inspiration, as the papists are where to
fix their wonderful infallibility. For if we suppose
that this inspiration is confined to any one of the
several sects that use extemporary prayer, we pre-
scribe to the Holy Spirit, and limit him with a wit-
ness, and shall be sadly perplexed to determine to
which particular party this wonderful privilege is
given. If we suppose that this privilege is common to the ministers of all the sects, then we must
conclude that the Holy Ghost inspires opposite petitions to men of opposite principles, and directs
one sect to pray against another: for instance, if
he inspires the Burghers * to pray against the principles of their seceding brethren the Antiburghers,
and to cut them off from their communion by ex-
communication; we cannot suppose that he inspires
the Antiburghers to return the compliment : and if
he inspires the ministers of these sects to pray against
the principles of the church established by law, he
does not direct the ministers of the established
church, in their public prayers, to call the secession
a dangerous schism : that the ministers of the seve-

* Burgher and Antiburgher are the names of two parties
among the Scotch seceders, taken from the cause of their
quarrel, an oath imposed in some of the royal burroughs in
Scotland upon those they admit into the corporation.

ra]

ral fects do pray for the fuccefs of their feveral parties, and that God would hinder the fpreading of
the principles of the other fects, is evident to all
the world.   Now, unlefs we would be guilty of the
boldeft blafphemy, and fay that the Holy Ghoft
chimes in with the principles of the parfon, whatever they be (as the people are forced to do), we
muft conclude that this infpiration is not granted
but to one of the fects; and I fhall only requeft each
of them to ufe a form of prayer, until they fhall
be able to prove that this gift of infpiration belongs
to them.—And that the eftablifhed church, with
which I have to do, may be more willing to hear
and grant my requeft, I will produce fome ftrong
prefumptions that it does not belong to them: indeed the inftances that I have given above, are
more than fufficient for this purpofe; but I fhall
further add, firft, that if the confeffion of faith be
true, none of our minifters are infpired in their
prayers; for there all mankind are divided into two
claffes, the elect and the reprobates; yet it is evident beyond all poffibility of difpute, that the elect
pray as if it were poffible that they may be damned; and the reprobates as if it were poffible that
they may be faved; and yet it is impoffible that
the Holy Spirit infpires either of them with thefe
prayers, unlefs we be fo impious as to imagine that
he directs them to pray upon falfe principles, and
infpires them to pray for or againft what he knows
can never happen; and though fome of you urge
this argument of infpiration againft your adver-
faries, yet our church has in fact very fairly dif-
claimed it, by publifhing and authorifing a directory for public prayer; unlefs we would fuppofe
them fo prefumptuous as to direct the Holy Spirit
how to pray. In truth, our prefbyterian infpiration, is as myfterious and as uielefs a gift as the

D   popifh

popifh infallibility. The popifh church has an infallibility lodged fomewhere, but fhe knows not
where to find it in time of need; we prefbyterians
have an infpiration among us, but we know not to
which of all the fects it belongs. The infallible
church is filled with difputes, which her infallibility
cannot determine; and the infpired church has
nonfenfe, contradiction, and whimfical opinions,
vented in her public prayers, which her infpiration
does not prevent; the infallible church has the
moft unreafonable and abfurd creed of any church
upon earth; and the infpired church has, and will
have (while fhe adheres to her prefent plan), a
very defective, unreafonable, and dangerous kind
of public worfhip: and fully, and juftly, does the
Providence of heaven confute the vain pretenfions
of prefumptuous men.

BUT it may be faid, and it has been faid, that
this gift of infpiration is not univerfal to all our
minifters, nor uniform and conftant to any of them,
but granted now and then by fits and ftarts, fomething (I fuppofe) like the quakers fpirit. I cannot help thinking, if this be the cafe, that the
quakers proceed more judicioufly than we; they patiently wait in filence till they feel, or imagine they
feel the influences of the Spirit; but if he does
not come, we venture to do without him: they
humbly fubmit to his will, to infpire whom he
pleafeth; but we confine him to the minifter: they
ftop fhort when his influence ceafes: but we run
our glaffes, let his influences ceafe when they will.
I would therefore humbly propofe, either that, like
quakers, we fhould wait the Spirit, and permit any
one of the congregation, who chanced to be infpired, to dictate our devotions; or that a form of
prayer be compofed and authorifed, only to be ufed
when the minifter feels no infpiration. Let him
                                                    have

have full liberty to depart from the form, when he f ls upon his mind the miraculous influences of t e Holy Spirit fuggefting the matter of his prayers. By this method, we fhall gain two very confiderable advantages; firft, we fhall always worfhip, either by infpiration or by an approved form, and be certain (unlefs the parfon deceives us), that the ignorance, affectation, ill-timed zeal, pride, or paffions of the man himfelf, cannot tincture our public worfhip, or mix themfelves with our prayers. And next, we fhall difcover when our parfons are infpired; for, as things are managed at prefent, this miracle is as much loft in our prefbyterian church, as the famous miracle of tranfubftantiation is among the papifts. In both churches there is a wonderful manifeftation of almighty power, yet no one is able to perceive it in either. The papifts are convinced that bread and wine are converted into flefh and blood, though to all the fenfes they remain bread and wine ftill; we prefbyterians are perfuaded that our minifters are fometimes infpired, though we cannot tell when the infpiration begins or ends; and though our minifters in this cafe, lie under the fame misfortune that Hudibras did,

When with greateft art he fpoke,
You'd think, he talked like other folk:

fo it unluckily fares with them; when they pray moft by infpiration, they only pray like other people; and all my attention and fkill has never been able to difcover the infpiration in one fingle inftance. But by the method that I am propofing, we fhall difcover that the infpiration immediately begins, when the minifter departs from the eftablifhed form, and perhaps we may make another difcovery; I mean, that the rage of party, the fpirit

of

of pride and enthufiafm, as frequently infpire our minifters, as the fpirit of peace and love. In a word, let thofe minifters who have pride enough to believe, and prefumption to affirm that they are infpired, and can find people fo ignorant and credulous as to believe them, or fo tame and indifferent as to truft their devotions to an imaginary infpiration, let thefe I fay, ufe the prefent method, but have pity upon us who fee the difficulty, difadvantages, and great danger of our prefent way of worfhip.

As we cannot find in fcripture any promife of fuch a gift, as we are convinced that there can be no need of it (unlefs we fuppofe that the Holy Ghoft has not fully revealed the will of God for our falvation); as we are abfolutely certain that you are not all infpired, and have no reafon to believe that any one of you is fo; we prefume moft humbly and moft earneftly to requeft, that fome pious form of prayer may be compofed and authorifed. The only infpiration that is promifed in fcripture, that is neceffary or that can be ufeful, is that the Holy Spirit will infpire the hearts of the faithful with affections proper for this important duty; fuch as fhame and forrow in confeffion, an humble chriftian hope of obtaining what we afk in our petitions, gratitude and love in our thankfgiving, and fuch other affections as are fuitable to the feveral parts of prayer; and no man I believe will fay that the Holy Spirit cannot, or prove that he will not, infpire our hearts with thefe affections, as eafily and as readily when we pray by a form, as when we pray without one. And as far as prayer may be confidered as one of the means of infpiring thefe affections, a form feems better calculated to anfwer that purpofe, in public affemblies, than extemporary effufions: for in the extempore

way,

way, the hearer (if he has any fenfe of the nature and importance of prayer) muft begin the duty with a trembling heart, and go through it with a continual diffidence, as he trufts it entirely to the difcretion of another man; fometimes to a man whom he never faw before, and always to a man who has not fo much as calmly confidered it himfelf. He muft often fufpend his affent, when he is not fatisfied of the propriety of the expreffion; he muft lofe the fenfe, where the fentence is intricate, and through the whole, be in perplexity, fufpicion, fear, and real danger. Whereas when prayers are offered by a form, no word needs efcape him, he underftands every word, he perceives the connection of every fentence; and let the minifter's judgment be ever fo weak, his learning ever fo little, his manner of expreffing himfelf perplexed, his principles pernicious, his paffions ever fo keen, and his party prejudices ever fo violent, yet in fpite of all thefe he offers a reafonable fervice, and breathes forth the warm feelings of his foul, in decent, devout, heart-affecting, and heart-approved prayers. This obfervation may in a great meafure obviate the fecond objection; I mean that a form of prayer does not fo much enliven the devotion of the people; but I beg leave further to obferve, that they who are ufed to worfhip in the extemporary way cannot be competent judges in this cafe; becaufe they have not fairly made the experiment, but reafon only from fpeculation. When they drop into a place where forms are ufed, they come in with ftrong prejudices, they are entire ftrangers to the form, and are perplexed in all the parts of it.—It happens with them in this cafe, as it does with men in every other thing, what they have not been accuftomed to, appears ftrange, what they are unacquainted with, feems perplexed,

and

and what they do not know reafons for, is apt to appear unreafonable. It may be too, that the ignorant mifs the unnatural cant, the frantic geftures, and fearful diftortions of the face, that in their opinion are effential parts of prayer. But let a man of fenfe and candour, make himfelf mafter of a form, and try the experiment for a year or two, by attending carefully to prayers offered in that way; and then and not till then, will he be able to determine whether the form, or the extemporary method, has the nobleft effect to enliven his devotions. At leaft it is certain, that many who have tried both, give their opinion in favour of a form; and that they who ufe a form of prayer, conftantly affirm that they feel it ten times more enlivening, and better calculated to infpire devout affections, than extemporary effufions. And there muft be fomething in it, becaufe the profeffors of all religions under the fun have chofen this method; the chriftian church univerfally ufed it till the fifteenth century, and indeed may be faid to do fo at prefent, for we make fuch a fmall part of the catholic church, that our practice hardly deferves to be confidered as an exception

I fhall not dwell long upon the fpeculative arguments that are offered by either fide, becaufe ingenious men will always find fomething plaufible to fay in defence of a practice that anfwers their purpofes. They who ufe forms, fay that their minds are free from all diftraction, and fear, and have nothing elfe to do but attend to the object of their prayers, and maintain upon their minds a conftant and lively fenfe of the importance of the bufinefs in which they are engaged, free from the care of examining every fentence before they offer it as their petition; fecure that no indecent or unchriftian expreffion can mix with their devotions,

being

being already fatisfied of the propriety of the whole form. They fay that the mind of man is not able to attend to many things at once, and that in our way of worfhip, if the people offer a reafonable fervice, they muft examine every fentence, hear every word, and underftand every word they hear; that they muft remember what went before, if they would conceive the connexion, that they muft unravel what is expreffed in a perplexed manner, if they would pray with judgment; and in fine, that they muft give their Amen to their prayers, with a more fuperficial examination of them, and a much lefs perfect knowledge of their contents, than they would venture to fet their fubfcription to an addrefs to their fuperiors upon earth.

WE anfwer, that the novelty and variety of the expreffion in our extemporary method, help to fix the mind and keep up the attention. They afk us, upon what is the mind fixed, upon the object and matter of our prayers, or upon the novelty and variety of expreffion? If we fay upon the object and matter of our prayers, they will tell us, that there are in thefe, neither novelty nor variety to affift us; becaufe our prayers are always addreffed to that Being who is *the fame to-day, yefterday, and for ever*; and the matter of our prayers in public muft always be nearly the fame: but if our minds be fixed upon the variety of the expreffion, or novelty of the phrafe, they fay (and I fear they fpeak truth) that this is not prayer, but mere amufement; fuch as the mind receives from mufic, a fong, or an entertaining piece of hiftory; that it might per-haps prepare the mind for prayer, but is not prayer any more than a fermon is prayer.

IT is evident that many of our minifters are fenfible, that their people attend only to the out-ward circumftances of their prayers, and that the

way

way to be popular is to tickle their ears with ftrange founds, or pleafe their eyes with antic geftures ; elfe why do many of them affect fuch an unmanly whining cant? Why ufe fuch difmal heavy tones, and draw out their words to fuch an immoderate length? Or why do they affect fuch diftortions in their faces? All the world will acknowledge, that thefe are neither neceffary nor ufeful parts of prayer, unlefs to pleafe the filly vulgar, who regard little more than the found and circumftances of our prayers.

But whatever weight may be in the fpeculative arguments upon either fide, experience and matter of fact are fairly againft us ; for they who fay that forms of prayer enliven devotion, feem, by a certain decency obfervable amongft them in time of fervice, to confirm what they fay ; while the vifible inattention and indifference of our congregations, flatly contradict our arguments, and prove to the very fenfes, that our extemporary prayers do not enliven our devotions. In affemblies where forms are ufed, there is at leaft the appearance of devotion, and an air of ferioufnefs. None of them are feen fleeping in time of fervice, few of them gazing about them, not one of them ever prefumes (unlefs in a cafe of abfolute neceffity) to remove till the whole fervice be ended ; and they frequently meet in public for the bufinefs of prayer, which * Mr. Fordyce juftly complains we never do, and feems to think that it would be very difficult to perfuade our people to it. Thus the practice of thofe who ufe forms of prayer, proves to me more effectually than all the fpeculative arguments that can be offered, that they have an higher opinion of the great duty of public prayer, feel a greater pleafure from it, or are fome way or

* Edification by public Inftitutions.

other

other more affected by it, than our people are.
Whereas in our affemblies there is not fo much as
the air of devotion, not even the outward appearance of ferioufnefs and attention? many are fleeping, more gazing about them, and all of *them* †
betray a vifible impatience till prayer is over, that they
may be entertained with fomething more to their liking.
When fermon is over do we not fee them remove in
crowds, tho' one half of our fervice, and that the
moft folemn half, ftill remains? Perhaps it may be
thought, that this is not a fair account of the matter, and that I mifreprefent things. Will you believe your own brethren? they fhall vouch what I
have faid; let us firft hear Mr. Bennet's report of the
devotion of our brethren in England §; " That carelefs air (fays he) which fits upon the face of a congregation, when engaged in prayer, fhews, how
little they know of the matter, and how few ferioufly
join in public and folemn prayer; fome gaze about
them, others fall afleep——others fix their eye it
may be on the minifter, and are affected with what
he fays; but then they only hear him pray, and are
moved with the prayer, juft as they hear fermons
and are moved thereby (a moft lively picture of our
public worfhip!)—— I muft profefs to you, fhould
the enemies of our way of worfhip be prefent to
obferve us, there is nothing I fhould be fo much
afhamed of, as our exceeding carelefs, irreverent,
indevout manner of joining in public prayer." So
far Mr. Bennet bears witnefs to the want of devotion in congregations in England, where extemporary prayers are ufed. Let us now fee if this
way of worfhip, has any better fuccefs or happy
effects amongft us here in Scotland. Alas it is

† Edification by public Inftitutions.
§ Sermon upon joining in public prayer, p. 112.

every

every where the fame unnatural, unreafonable, life-
lefs thing. Let Mr. Fordyce fpeak for the Scotch
congregations: " I doubt not my brethren (fpeak-
ing to the clergy) but you have frequently obferved
when the minifter of God has been addreffing him
in the name, and as the mouth of the people,
the greateft part of them feem to be doing any
thing, rather than joining in folemn fervice; in
reality there is no exercife of a fpiritual nature
which the generality feem to regard fo little, or to
attend fo liftlefsly; feem did I fay, the expreffion is
much too feeble; their infenfibility, their irreverence
in this refpect are, from the whole of their deport-
ment, moft fhamefully diftinguifhable and fla-
grant." * If this be true, as indeed it is the very
truth, I may be allowed to add, that it is moft
fhamefully impudent in us to alledge that forms of
prayer deaden the devotion of th people, and that
our extemporary method enlivens it. The little
refpect, nay vifible contempt, that our peope fhew
of public prayers, prove more clearly than all fpeculative arguments that can be offered, that our prefent way of worfhip is very ill calculated for enlivening the devotion of the people: I have proved by
two unexceptional witneffes, and had it been con-
fiftent with the brevity I propofed, could have produced many more, to prove, that our devotion is
not only dead, but wants even all appearance of
life. In truth it needs no proof, for every Sunday
will fhew that we want attention, and reverence, to
this moft important duty; and every impartial
heart will tell its owner (if he underftands the nature of prayer), that it is very difficult to join in
our public worfhip as it is at prefent performed;
that it is impoffible to do it rationally; that it cannot

* Edification by public Inftitutions.

be

be attempted without great danger; and that in fact he does it very seldom, and even then in a very faint and lifeless manner.

ALLOW me next to confider the third objection offered againft forms of prayer. I mean that the wants of a congregation cannot be fo fully expreffed in that way, as by the extemporary method. This objection fuppofes, that a number of the moft learned and pious men of the age (for fuch I imagine would be employed) deliberately compofing a form of prayer, calmly recollecting the matter of it, frequently reviewing the whole, furnifhed with all the antient and modern liturgies, directed by all that has been written on the fubject, and affifted by every one that wifhes well to religion and virtue, are more likely to omit fome neceffary petition, than a fingle perfon perhaps of very indifferent talents, and a very moderate education, trufting entirely to an extemporary invention, and to his own memory. The man who can fuppofe this, hardly deferves to be reafoned with; for it is evident, that, in the firft cafe, our prayers will be brought as near perfection as poffible; that in the fecond, many things muft be omitted, many injudicioufly expreffed, many needlefsly repeated, and the whole tinctured with weaknefs, paffions, and party principles of the fpeaker, and that his beft performances will be as much inferior to a general form of prayer, as he himfelf is in difcretion, learning, and judgment, to the greateft men that have wrote upon the fubject, and to a number of men of the beft hearts, and calmeft, ableft heads, conveened to compofe the form. The wants, and confequently the matter of the petitions of a chriftian congregation, muft in the main be always the fame; they will at all times have fins to confefs, ftill have need to afk pardon, and to implore the divine grace to direct their thoughts, words, and actions; it will ever be their
duty

duty, to pray for all ranks of men, &c. If any general calamity fhould happen, fuch as war, famine, or peftilence, proper forms may be provided ; in private cafes, perhaps it might be more for the honour of our religion, and decency of our worfhip that we did not defcend to the particular circumftances, fo much as we do. It is needlefs to defcribe the difeafe to an omnifcient God ; moft cafes of this nature, might be comprehended under the general names of ficknefs and diftrefs; but if it be thought proper to deal with God Almighty as we do with an ordinary doctor, and to lay the cafe before him at full length, methods may be found to indulge the humour of the clergy, in this refpect, without leaving our whole worfhip to their difcretion, and putting all our public petitions in their power.

SHOULD the fpiritual condition of a congregation be altered (if it poffibly can alter fo much, that the eftablifhed form could not comprehend the cafe, which in my humble opinion cannot happen, if the form be well compofed) let the prefbytery, fynod, or commiffion of the affembly be applied to, and the cafe being calmly confidered, its nature and tendency deliberately examined, and its truth and certainty afcertained ; let a form of prayer be compofed fuitable to the cafe : but this is too delicate, too dangerous, and difficult an affair, to be trufted to the difcretion or capacity of any one clergyman ; for weaknefs, or villainy, in this refpect, has more than once difhonoured our public prayers, with the groffeft enthufiafm, perverted them to ferve very bad purpofes, and expofed the moft folemn part of our fervice, as well as religion itfelf, to the ridicule of infidels.

IN a word, the ordinary wants of a chriftian congregation may, nay muft be more fully expreffed by
a form

a form of prayer, than by extempore effufions : and extraordinary cafes, after they are difcovered and examined, may eafily be provided for, and it is not only poffible, but very eafy, to provide for all cafes that ought to be particularly mentioned in our pub-lic prayers, in the firft compofition of them. But to prevent all wrangling upon this fubject, and (if poffible) to content the moft felf-fufficient clergyman, let there be a proper place in this propofed form of prayer, where the minifter may have liberty to pray for all extraordinary cafes, in what words he thinks proper. It is better, that a fmall part of our wor-fhip be expofed to the indifcretion, ignorance, and paffions of the parfon, than that the whole fhould be liable, as it is at prefent, to be made the pro-perty of faction, to be tinctured with the prejudices and whimfical opinions of every private minifter, and offered upon the pernicious principles of the deift, or the extravagant notions of the enthufiaft.

I shall not dwell long upon the laft objection, I mean that forms of prayer are unlawful, becaufe I believe it never will be offered by men of fenfe or learning; and it is lofing time and pains to reafon with fuch as are deftitute of both. I fhall only beg leave to obferve, that they who fay that forms of prayer are unlawful, in fact fay, that God Almighty commanded, that our Saviour attended, ufed, and taught his difciples an unlawful way of worfhip; for that he did fo, I have proved already, and our own directory for public worfhip acknowleges that " Our Lord's prayer is not only a pattern for prayer; but itfelf a moft comprehenfive prayer." Here I cannot help obferving with regret, that wherever our directory directs well, there our clergy have defpifed our directory; for inftance, it recom-mends that the Lord's prayer be ufed in our public worfhip; that ordinarily a chapter out of each Tefta-ment be read at every meeting: the firft is neglected
by

by moſt, and the laſt by all of them. It directs that our
worſhip begin with prayer, but now it begins with
praiſe ; that the miniſter before worſhip ſhall ſolemnly
exhort the people to the worſhiping of the great name
of God ; but at preſent we ruſh into a very ſolemn part
of worſhip, without a word of previous exhortation,
and I fear very often without a ſerious thought.   It
is eaſy to find out the reaſon why the Lord's prayer
and the reading of the ſcriptures have been joſtled
out of our ſervice ; they have been forced out to
make room for Maſs John's *more maſterly performances*;
but why the other alterations have been made, the
clergy, who directs all things, can only tell. To them
I leave it, and reſume my ſubject.   If forms are
unlawful, we are unlawfully baptized, for that is
done by a form ; and all the extemporary prayers
which we uſe upon that occaſion are not eſſential to
the ſacrament, and are additions of men.   We ad-
miniſter the Lord's ſupper in an unlawful manner,
for we do it by a form, I mean the words of the
firſt inſtitution : we are diſmiſſed every Lord's day
with an unlawful bleſſing ; for one of the ſolemn
forms with which the apoſtles conclude their e-
piſtles, is always uſed upon that occaſion : ſo that
nothing can be more inconſiſtent with ingenuity and
common ſenſe, than for us to cry out againſt forms,
when the moſt ſolemn and important parts of our
religion and woſhip are performed in that way, and
when we neither baptize, nor communicate, nor
bleſs our congregations in a lawful way, unleſs forms
be lawful ; nor do theſe things in the beſt manner,
unleſs doing them by a form be the beſt.

But further, If forms of prayer be not acceptable to God, and an uſeful way of worſhip for our-
ſelves, we groſly offend every time that we meet
in church : for it is impoſſible to ſing eighteen
or twenty lines of a pſalm, but we offer ſome
important

important petition by a form; and fome pfalms might be pointed out that are almoft continued prayers; fo that unlefs we will affirm, that our prayers are acceptable to God, and ufeful to our-felves when they are furg, but otherwife when they are faid by a form, we muft allow that we are in-confiftent with ourfelves when we cry out againft forms; and that our minifters impofe upon us, when they fpirit us up againft that way of worfhip, that they may have the better opportunity to gratify their own vanity, to manufacture our prayers after their own manner, and to mix them up with their own private opinions.

If extemporary worfhip be preferable, what good reafon can be given why the minifters do not fing pfalms extempore in our names, as well as offer ex-temporary prayers? for we are as much concerned to join in the laft as in the firft; a blunder in the one is as dangerous as in the other, and we could as well go along with him in our hearts, when he fung an extemporary pfalm, as we can do when he fays an extemporary prayer. This inconfiftency in our worfhip has not entirely efcaped the obfervation of our bethren, for many of them have warmly in-fifted upon it, that the Spirit of *God is reftrained by ufing the pfalms of David* *, and therefore propofed, that we fhould fing as well as pray extempore: and upon the fuppofition, that public worfhip in the extemporary way is moft rational, they were cer-tainly in the right; for no good reafons can be given for praifing God by forms, that will not be equally good for praying to him in the fame way; and no objection can be offered againft the laft, that will not be as ftrong againft the firft; for inftance, if we fay that praying to God by forms deadens the devotion of the people, fo will praifing him by

* Heylin's hiftory of the prefbyterians.

forms

forms too. If forms of prayer reftrain the influences of the Holy Spirit, fo muft forms of praife. If forms of prayer cannot exprefs all the wants of a chriftian congregation, neither will forms of praife comprehend all the caufes for which a chriftian congregation may have reafon to praife God; efpecially, as the forms we ufe were compofed feveral thoufand years ago, and calculated chiefly for the Jewifh religion and worfhip. If forms of prayer be unlawful in themfelves, fo muft our forms of praife, becaufe, as I have obferved before, they are often real prayers.

Supposing that extemporary worfhip was more acceptable to God, and ufeful to ourfelves, no man in a congregation can reap the benefit of it but the parfon. Our laity are moft grofly miftaken, if they imagine that they pray extempore by our prefent method; for if they pray in the words of the minifter (and in his words they muft pray if they join at all in public worfhip), they are as much confined to a form as any other people. For example, if the minifter fays, *moft gracious God forgive us our fins, preferve us from danger, and provide for our neceffities*; if the people repeat thefe words, either in their minds, or with their mouths, or both, it is evident that they pray as much by a form, as if the prayer had been compofed a thoufand years ago; in fact it is impoffible for a congregation to join in worfhip otherways than by a form; and all the difference is, that we worfhip by a form with which we are entirely unacquainted; a form that we have never feen nor examined before; a form that is trufted to the difcretion and ability of the parfon for the time, and which the minifter himfelf has never once read over, nor examined, even in the flighteft manner. It is hard to determine whether his prefumption in putting a

form

form of a prayer into our mouths, that he has never examined, or our complaisance in using a form that neither we nor our minister have ever once read over, is most unaccountable. But that either we or he should imagine, that to worship God in this manner is most rational for us, or most acceptable to him, is such an instance of the strength of prejudice, and the effects of education, as no man could have thought possible, had it not been proved by experience. For in fact, it is to imagine that our worship is the more rational, the more we are strangers to the words and matter of our prayers, and the whole access we have had to satisfy ourselves of the property of our petitions, and the more confidence we repose in another man.

THAT our worship will be the more acceptable to the Deity, the less care and pains that is taken about the words or matter of it by the parson, or the people, and that our prayers will be so much the sooner heard, the less chance they have to be expressed in proper words, or to consist of pious and reasonable petitions. We may sometimes have a better, or worse form according to the judgment and capacity of the minister, but we must always have a very defective one, and our very best form must be as far inferior to a national well-composed liturgy, as the learning, judgment, and memory of the one man, is to the abilities and calm reflection of a number of the most learned and judicious men of the age. I must confess that I have often beheld with indignation the parson pulling out his papers for the sermon, when he trusted the prayer to his invention and memory; not that I have any prejudice against reading of sermons, or am not convinced that it is the best method, unless the minister be a man of extraordinary parts, of extensive learning, and blessed with a very good

E
memory;

memory; but that I look upon it as an affront offered to God and the congregation, and very absurd in this instance, as it shews that the minister is less concerned about the propriety and decency of his address to his God, than to his people; and that he is more afraid of a blunder in his sermon, than in his worship; or at least, that he thinks, either that a mistake in the last is of less consequence than in the first, or that it is an easier matter to pray than to preach well. I own that he has reason to believe that any thing like a prayer will pass with the bulk of the people, because in truth they do not regard it much; but this should never induce him to shew that he is as careless about the matter and words of their prayers as they are themselves, and that he takes more care and pains to please them by his sermons, than to offer their prayers in a concise and proper manner.

I have often heard the members of our church, when the difficulties and dangers of our present way of worship have been fairly laid before them, satisfy themselves by saying, that most of our ministers had a form of prayer which they used, and with which, by length of time, their people became very well acquainted. I believe it may be true, that most of them naturally fall into a form; but, if we will believe themselves (and they certainly know the best) it is rather by chance than by design, and of consequence more by good luck, than good management, or much care, if the form they fall into be a good one. However, it is here granted, that the worshiping God by a form, is not only lawful and reasonable, but also necessary; and if this be case, why should not our worship be rendered uniform by an established general form of prayer? why should it not be brought as near perfection as possible, by the judgment, piety, and
learning

learning of our ableft minifters, and other members of our church, conferring together upon the fubject? why fhould not this form of prayer be communicated to the laity, that we may examine and approve of it? is the parfon's form fuch a fecret that we may not fee and examine it for ourfelves? is it an advantage to our worfhip that he may alter, curtail, or enlarge it, as his paffions or prejudices chance to direct, and warp into his form any whimfical opinions that he chances to embrace? we muft, notwithftanding of his form, go to the church with a trembling heart, as we know not but fome minifter may officiate whofe form of prayer we never have heard, our own minifter may have changed his, or fome unlucky and indecent petition may be thrown in, as he has it in his power to do as he pleafes.

At the fame time it is true, that our minifters, who carefully compofe and conftantly ufe a form of prayer, do as much as they can, in their prefent circumftances, to render our worfhip pure and rational, and to affift the devotions of their people; and therefore deferve their efteem and thanks; but yet it is evident, that thefe private forms have no great chance of being fo full and perfect, and that they have but few of the advantages of a general eftablifhed form of prayer, and many of the difadvantages of the extemporary method.

It has been often urged in defence of extempore public prayers, that the apoftles ufed that way of worfhip. If they did fo, they did more than their mafter either taught them, or gave them an example of, as far as we can judge. But fuppofing that it were proved (which it has not yet been, and I doubt never will be) that the apoftles ufed extemporary public prayer, I am afraid, we fhall not be able to infer from thence, that our minifters

E 2   fhould

should pray extempore, or that the people should trust every one of them with the composition, and direction of their public worship; unless it could be also proved, that every one of them is directed by immediate inspiration. I have often blushed for our ministers, when I have heard them urge this argument, as it is so weak and inconclusive in itself, and betrays so much presumption and self-sufficiency in them; for in fact it is putting our present ministers upon a level with the apostles. Some days ago I was passing by Bedlam, and observed one of its wretched inhabitants wrestling with a great iron gate; I asked him what he was about? he told me, with an air of importance, that his name was Sampson, and that he meant to carry up that gate to the top of an opposite hill, as his name-sake did the gate of Gaza. I did not stay to convince him that Sampson was endued with miraculous strength, but I could not help thinking that there was a great resemblance in his way of reasoning, or rather running mad, to the argument in hand; for the apostles were endued with miraculous gifts as much superior to the abilities of our present ministers, as Sampson's strength was to that of the poor bedlamite: they lived in an age in which miraculous gifts by the goodness of God were common in the church; but in our time there is nothing miraculous unless it be the self-sufficiency and presumption of the clergy, in taking upon them to offer an extemporary address to their Maker; and each of them claiming a right to make a whole parish pray as he pleases; and the absurd confidence reposed in them by the laity; and the tame submission by which they suffer every man that chances to fill their pulpits, to manufacture and mix up their prayers as he chuses. These indeed are miraculous things, such as no age, no country,

country, no religion, ever produced examples of;
and it is still more surprizing that the clergy themselves (as I have proved before) see, and publish
to the world, that the people do not join in public
worship; and the most learned and sensible part of
the laity feel and acknowledge that it is very difficult
and dangerous for them to join in it, as it is performed at present; and yet that none of our clergy
have compassion and humility to propose, nor any
of the laity resolution to demand   change, but
that all of them sit down with an abs'd and dangerous way of worship, introduced partly by ne-
cessity, and partly by enthusiasm, in the distract-
ed days of our reformation; disapproved of by
our ablest reformers from the beginning, as wit-
ness John Knox, who composed and used a form
of prayer; and only approved of and supported by
the silly ignorant vulgar, who have so little knowledge, either of the nature, or importance of
prayer, that they would not give themselves the
trouble to go to church, unless it were to hear a
sermon; and by the turbulent and self-sufficient
part of the clergy, who find that it gives them a fair
opportunity to sow discord, propagate faction, and
prostitute our worship to their foolish fondness for
popularity. That the mob who place great merit
in hearing many sermons, and think preaching the
most important part of public worship, should be
fond of our present method, is no wonder at all,
for our extemporary effusions are rather sermons
than prayers. It is natural too for the ambitious,
enthusiastical, and libertine part of our clergy to
be warmly attached to our present way of worship;
it most effectually answers their several purposes; it
affords the ambitious a large field for displaying
their popular talents, and an excellent opportunity to *preach themselves*; it gives enthusiasts and
libertines

libertines fair scope to vent their whimsical and pernicious principles: indeed nothing can be better calculated for propagating sedition, heresy, enthusiasm and party principles, than our present way of worship, since every minister has the composition of most of it, and the choice and management of the whole; so that it is no wonder if men of these characters be fond of it, nay it would be very surprizing if they could be persuaded to give up our present method.

But it is not easy to conceive why the learned, orthodox, and pious part of our clergy, who have no other views but the good of souls, and the glory of God, have not endeavoured to remedy these ills, by composing and authorizing such a form of prayer as might enable every congregation in the kingdom to offer their prayers upon truly christian principles: or how it comes to pass that the sensible and pious part of our laity (though they can hardly miss to see, that it is inconsistent with religion, and common sense, to trust the most solemn part of our worship to the discretion, honesty, and ability often of strangers whom they have never seen before, and always of individuals, of whose weakness and folly they have many instances) chuse to run such a terrible risk.

I have contributed my poor mite to deliver the laity from the hardships and danger to which they are exposed by our present way of worship; and as (I think) I have made it obvious, that the present method is attended with great inconveniencies and eminent danger to us poor lay men: I may likewise hope that the rulers of our church will lay our case to heart, and take such methods as may enable us to offer a rational service to the great source of reason, and to lift up holy hands without perplexity, fear, or danger. While our

case

continued as it is, our churches may indeed be
wded by thofe who have not fenfe to fee their
.nger, nor attention to perceive upon how many
oppofite principles they are made to pray ; perfons
who have never perhaps in all their lives reflected
upon the nature and importance of prayer, and
come to church partly becaufe it is the cuftom, or
at moft to hear a fermon ; but they who confider
the nature and importance of public worfhip will
hardly chufe, in a thing of fo great confequence,
to be blindfolded and led by the parfon.

WITH all humility and due deference I fubmit
the whole to your confideration, more extenfive
learning, and better judgment, and to the candid
reflection of all pious chriftians, and am, with the
greateft refpect,

Reverend Father,

your moft obedient,

and moft humble fervant,

Inverary,
May 8th, 1758.

A. T. Blackfmith.

FINIS.